PHONICS for the NEW READER

STEP-BY-STEP

by Harriette Fields ◇ illustrations by Anne Cox

Published by WORDS PUBLISHING
Copyright © 1991 by Harriette Fields
Copyright © 1991 illustrations by Anne Cox
Graphics by Tom Fields

Second Edition first printing
Printed and bound in the United States of America by:
Johnson Printing
Boulder, Colorado   3 3113 01270 2553

Library of Congress Catalog Card Number: 90-70334
ISBN: 0-9625802-1-x

Thanks to Joe,
  for getting me started.
Thanks to Abby & Christopher,
  for giving me a reason.
Thanks to Tom & Bill,
  for making it possible.

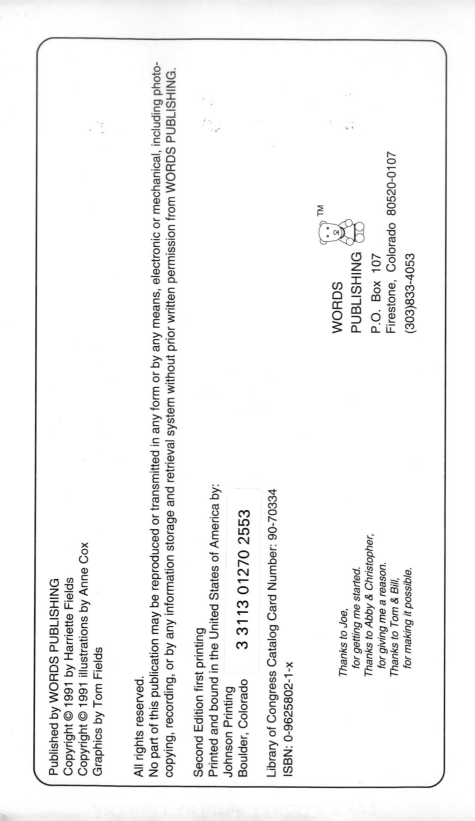

WORDS
PUBLISHING ™
P.O. Box 107
Firestone, Colorado 80520-0107
(303)833-4053

INTRODUCTION

PHONICS for the NEW READER easily fits into reading programs that are aimed at providing new readers with the necessary skills for an unlimited reading ability and vocabulary.

The clarity and simplicity of the phonics instruction in this book makes it easy for you to teach new readers that:

- an English alphabet letter has a name, shape and sound.
- words are spoken by synthesizing letter sounds.
- words are written, read and sounded from left to right.
- there are rules that govern the sounds that letters make.
- there are exceptions to the rules.

PHONICS for the NEW READER is divided into eight lessons that provide clear and simple explanation to your new readers, along with exercise in directly applying his or her phonics skills. The logical progression of the text allows your new readers to master the skills of one lesson and confidently move on to the next.

i

Your new reader will practice building one-syllable, short vowel words and learn how to turn short vowel words into long vowel words. After learning many special words and exceptions to the rules of phonics, your new reader will progress to making new sounds using consonant, vowel, special vowel and vowel-consonant combinations.

Phonics instruction is vital to the literacy of your new reader and **PHONICS for the NEW READER** will be of great assistance to you in delivering that instruction, clearly and simply.

HOW TO USE THIS BOOK

Begin with a daily 5 to 10 minute study session and allow your new reader to learn at his or her own pace. The length of your study session will increase as the skills of your new reader increases.

Read everything aloud to your new reader (except your instructions and example words) and run your finger under and along the words as you read, from left to right.

Follow the lessons in sequence and do not skip around. Your new reader must acquire the phonics skills of one lesson before moving on to the next.

TABLE OF CONTENTS

x

LESSON 1 - LETTER NAMES, SHAPES AND SOUNDS

Read pages 2, 3 and 4 to your new reader.

Following page 4 are the consonants and vowels in large black letters. An example word for the correct sound for each consonant and the short sound for each vowel is provided below the letter.

Beginning with the letter b, trace the letter with your finger and say to your new reader, "consonant letter b says "b". Then ask your new reader to trace the letter and say the letter name and sound. Move on to the consonant letter c and so on.

If your new reader has difficulty pronouncing a sound or distinguishing between similar sounds, face each other and show the correct placement of the tongue and lips.

When your new reader has mastered the sounds of the consonants and the short sounds of the vowels, move on to page14.

The Alphabet in Small Letters

These are the **small letters** in the **alphabet** of the **English Language.**

(point to the letter and say the letter name)

a b c d e f g h

i j k l m n o p q

r s t u v w x y z

Introducing Consonants

Each letter has a **name**, **shape** and **sound**.

First you will learn the **name**, **shape** and **sound** of the letters that are called **consonant letters.**

The word **consonant** is spelled:

c - o - n - s - o - n - a - n - t

continued...

See the consonant and
say its name.

Follow the arrows and
feel its shape.

Listen, and hear the sound
the consonant letter makes.

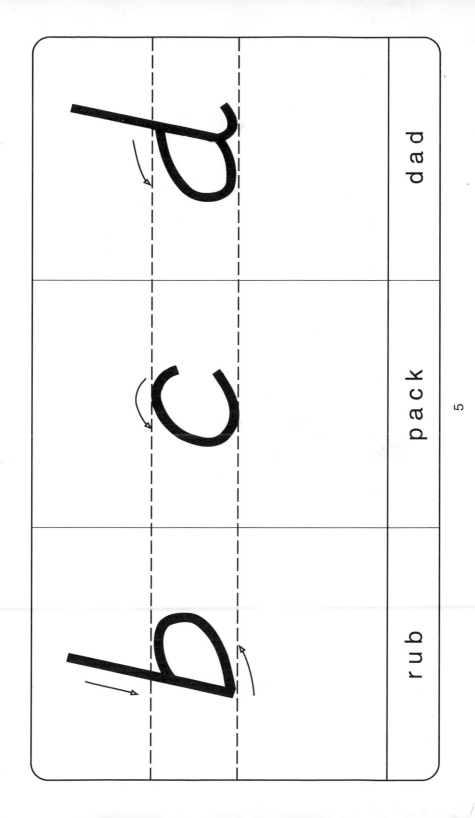

dad

pack

rub

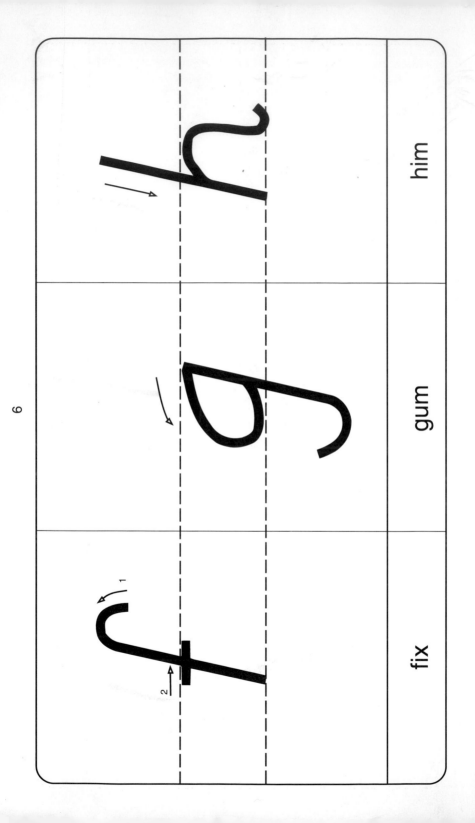

him

gum

fix

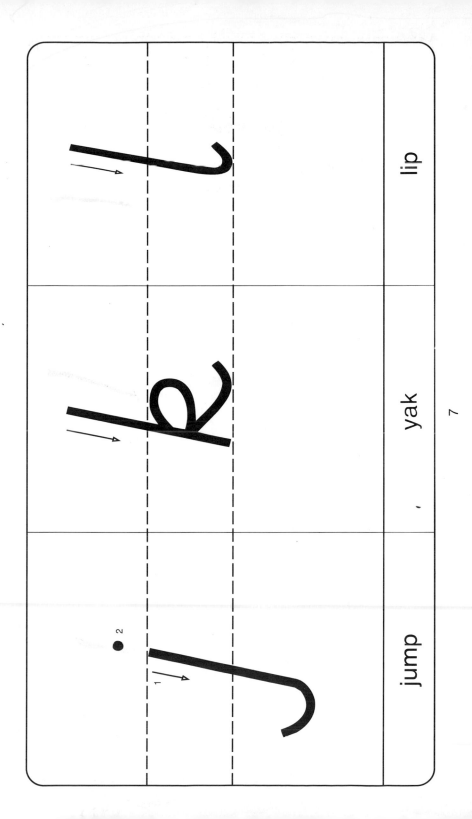

lip

yak

jump

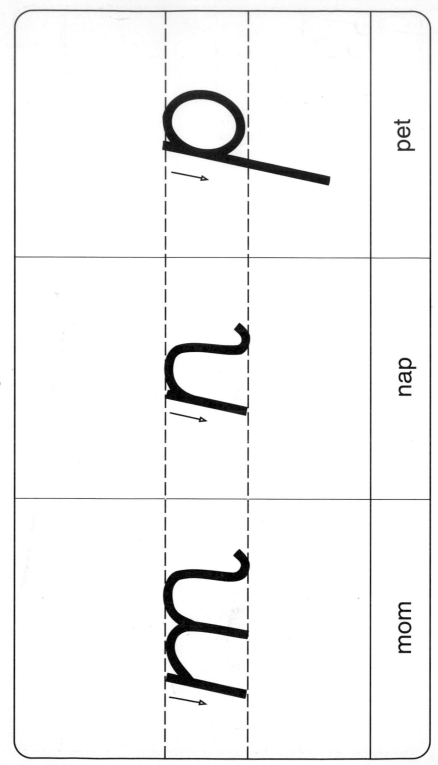

| pet | nap | mom |

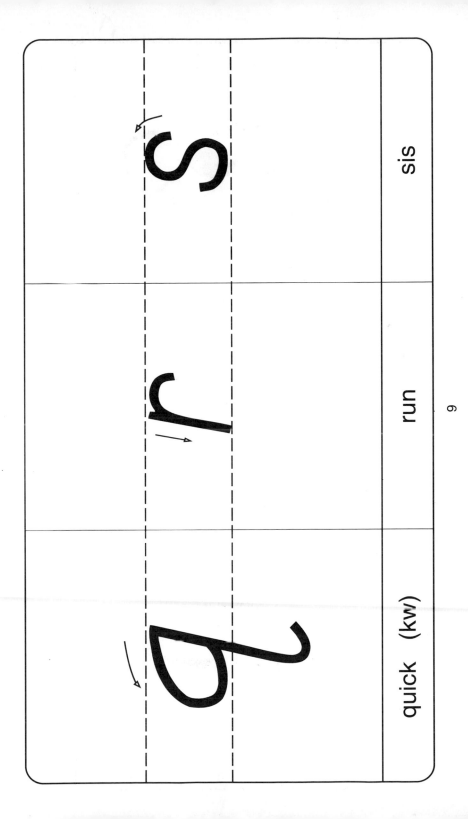

quick (kw)	run	sis

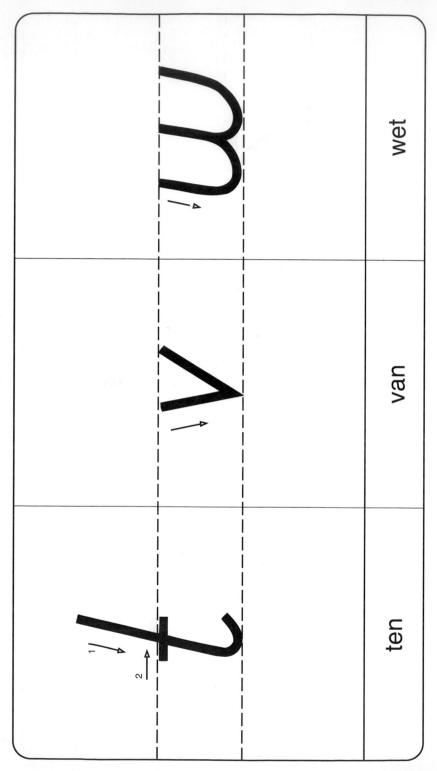

ten	van	wet

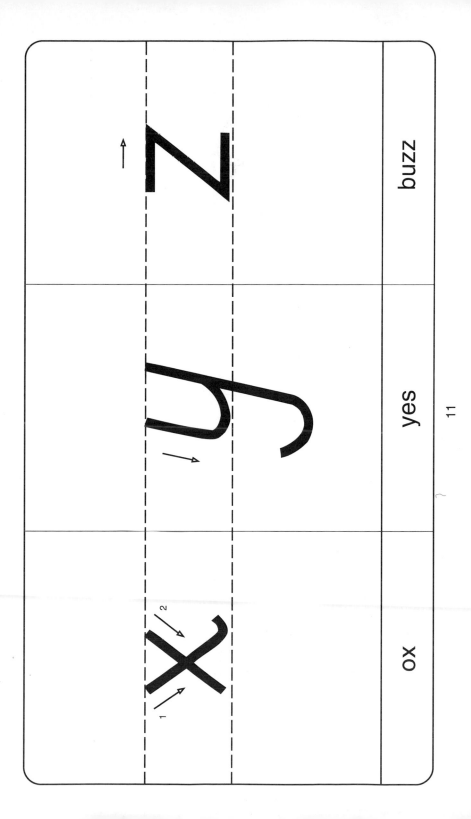

ox

yes

buzz

Introducing Vowels

Now you will learn the name, shape and **short** sounds of the letters that are called **vowel** letters.

See the vowel and say its name.

Follow the arrows and feel its shape.

Listen, and hear the **short** sound the **vowel** letter makes.

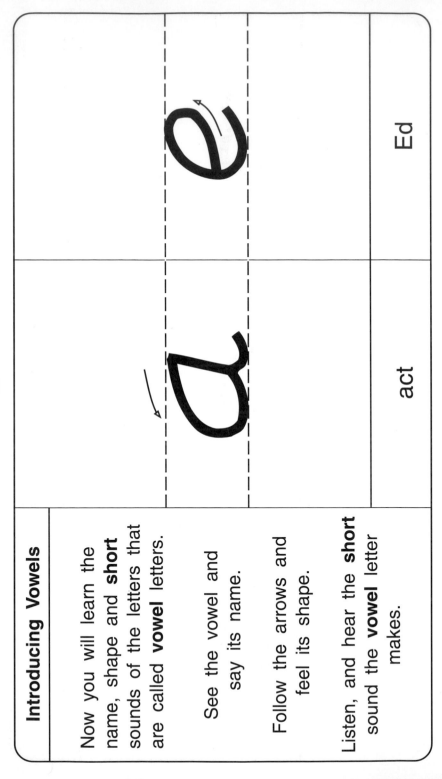

act

Ed

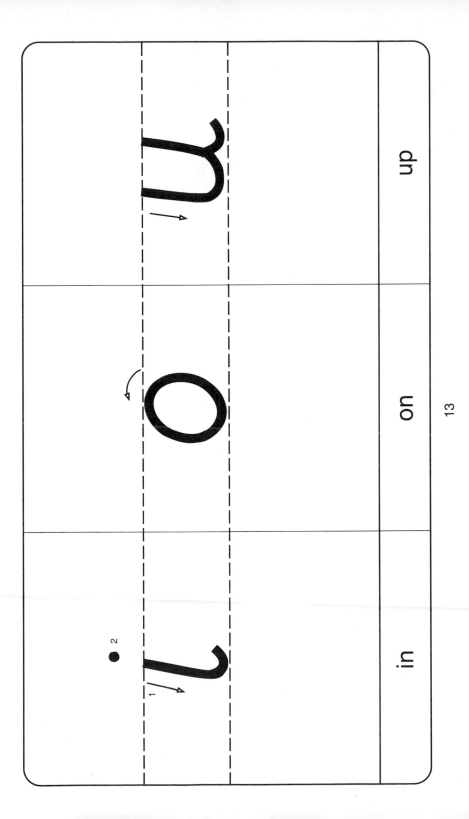

| in | on | up |

The Alphabet in Capital Letters

Each letter has **two shapes**. The **big letter** is called a **capital letter**.

The **capital letter** makes the same sound as its **small letter**.

A a B b C c D d E e F f G g H h

I i J j K k L l M m N n O o P p Q q

R r S s T t U u V v W w X x Y y

Z z

LESSON 2 - SHORT VOWELS

Your new reader will now begin word building.

Ask your new reader to spell, sound and blend the practice word.

Using a chalkboard or pencil and paper, ask your new reader to write the practice word.

When your new reader has mastered the phonics skills of this lesson, begin LESSON 3.

The Brēve and What It Tells You

This mark is called a **breve**. ⌣
The word **breve** is spelled:

b - r - e - v - e

When you see a **breve above** a **vowel** it tells you that the **vowel sound** is **short**.

What is the **short sound** of each **vowel**?

⌣ a   ⌣ e   ⌣ i   ⌣ o   ⌣ u

Spell, Sound and Blend

When you read a word, you always read from

left $\longrightarrow$ to $\longrightarrow$ **right**

When you say the letter **names**, you **spell** the word.

Now say the letter **names** and **spell** the word.

at

continued...

17

When you say the letter **sounds**, you **sound** the word.
Now say the letter **sounds** and **sound** the word.

ᵕ**at**

When you **blend** the sounds together, you **pronounce** the word.
Now **blend** the sounds together and **pronounce** the word.

ᵕ**at**

Practice Words Using a

( ) sat

( ) fat

( ) Sam

( ) can　　　( ) bat　　　( ) Dan

( ) mad　　　( ) cat　　　( ) had

( ) jag　　　　( ) jam　　　( ) wag

( )

( )

( )

( )

( )

Sam ran fast past Dan.

19

Practice Words Using e

◡ wet   ◡ hen   ◡ men

◡ yes   ◡ jet   ◡ get   ◡ best   ◡ pet

◡ Ted   ◡ went   ◡ fed   ◡ tent

◡ Meg and Ted can help Ed.

Practice Words Using i

⌣ Jim   ⌣ mix   ⌣ grin   ⌣ fix

⌣ win   ⌣ big   ⌣ skin   ⌣ pig

⌣ lip   ⌣ dig   ⌣ zip   ⌣ twig

⌣ Slim Jim can ⌣ skip and ⌣ swim.

21

Practice Words Using o

) hot

) frog

) soft

) dog

) fox

) mom

) box

) Tom

) stop

) Don

) drop

) Ron

) Kit's soft dog slips on wet sod.

Practice Words Using ꞈ u

⌣ hum   ⌣ jump   ⌣ drum   ⌣ bump

⌣ nut   ⌣ cup   ⌣ hut   ⌣ pup

⌣ hug   ⌣ cub   ⌣ plug   ⌣ tub

⌣   ⌣   ⌣   ⌣   ⌣   ⌣   ⌣

Ten plump skunks dug in big mud clumps.

LESSON 3 - LONG VOWELS

Continue word building.

When your new reader has mastered the phonics skills of this lesson, begin LESSON 4.

Long Vowels Say Their Name

The **vowels** make more than one sound.

You have learned the **short sound** of each **vowel**.
Now you will learn the **long sound** of each **vowel**.

When a **vowel** says its **name**, it has the **long sound**.
Say the **vowel name** and hear the **long sound**.

a   e   i   o   u

The Macron and What It Tells You

This mark is called a **macron**. ⎯⎯⎯

Spell the word **macron**.

m - a - c - r - o - n

When you see a **macron** above a **vowel**, it tells you the **vowel sound** is **long**.

What is the **long sound** of each **vowel**?

ā   ē   ī   ō   ū

27

Practice Words Using Long Vowels

The — tells you the vowel sound is long.

gō   nō   sō   hī !

bē   hē   mē   wē

       ā   ī   Ōh !

"Silent E"

E at the end of a word makes the **first vowel** in the word make the **long vowel sound**.

The **e** at the **end** does not make a sound. The **e** at the **end** is **silent**.

What is the **vowel** in this word?

at

continued...

29

What is the **first vowel** in this word?

ate

Does the **e** at the end make the **first vowel** sound, **long** or **short?**

Does the **e** at the end make a **sound?**

Spell, Sound and Blend:

āte

Practice Words Using ă and ā

) mad	¯ made	¯ fade
) cap	¯ cape	) fad
) Jan	¯ Jane	) tap
		¯ tape
	) Sam	¯ same

) Jan and ¯ Jane ¯ made a ¯ cake and ¯ ate it.

31

Practice Words Using ĭ and ī

⏑ hĭd   hīde   ⏑ rĭd   rīde

⏑ pĭp   pīpe   ⏑ rĭp   rīpe

⏑ kĭt   kīte   ⏑ bĭt   bīte

Ā drĭp from a pīpe went 'plŏp' and 'plĭp'.

Practice Words Using ŏ and ō

tot   tōte   nŏt   nōte

rŏd   rōde   rŏb   rōbe

hŏp   hōpe   mŏp   mōpe

Rŏb had ŏn a tan rōbe and rōde in a red hot-rod.

33

Practice Words Using ŭ and ū

ŭs

ūse   cŭt   ūcute

cŭb   cūbe

Sometimes the long u sound in a word says ōo (as in too).

tŭb   tūbe

Practice Words Using ā, ō and ī

sāve	gāze	wāve	hāze
hōme	nōse	dōme	rōse
fīre	tīme	wīre	dīme

A wīre in a tīre can make a tīre go flat.

35

Add d at the End

Spell, Sound and Blend:

use

gaze

Does the **e** at the end make a sound?
Now add **d** to the **end** of these words.

used

gazed

Practice Words Adding d at the End

bāke	bāked	wīpe	wīped
tāpe	tāped	tīme	tīmed
sāve	sāved	wāve	wāved

Jūne sat on a raft, rōde on a wāve and wāved a flag.

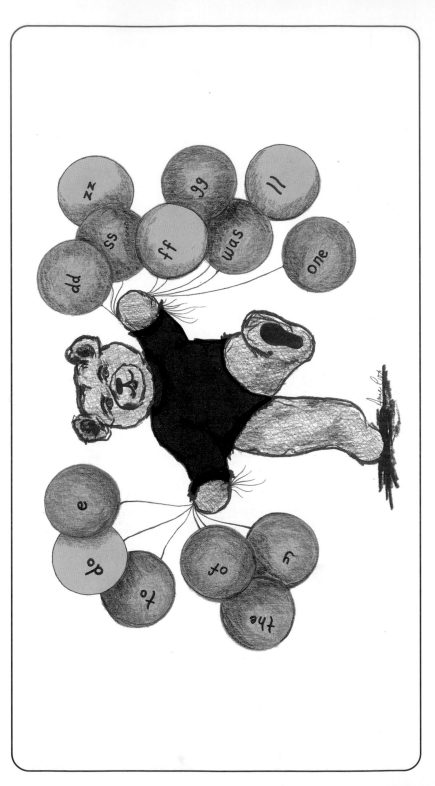

LESSON 4 - SPECIAL WORDS AND LETTERS

Continue word building.

When your new reader has mastered the phonics skills of this lesson, begin LESSON 5.

Y as Both Consonant and Vowel

Y is sometimes a **consonant** and is sometimes a **vowel**.

The **vowels** are:

a   e   i   o   u

and sometimes

y

When **y** is the **first letter** in a word, **y** is a **consonant**.

Spell, Sound and Blend

◯ **yes**   ◯ **yet**

◯ **Ken ran fast yet he came in last.**

41

When **y** is not the first letter in a word, **y** is a **vowel**.

What is the **vowel** in this word?

fly

When **y** is the only **vowel** in a word, **y** makes the **long i** sound.

Spell, Sound and Blend:

fly

Practice Words Using y as a Vowel

cry   by   dry   sky

my   try

My twin sis sat close by me and we sped
on a sled past Fred.

43

THE

When **consonants** t and h stand side - by - side in a word, the t and h combine to make a new sound.

Listen, and hear the sound that t and h make when they stand side - by - side.

th

What is the sound that **t** and **h** make when they stand **side - by - side**?

Spell, Sound and Blend:

th̄e

― ） ） ）
The red bud on the plant came up
― ） ） ― ―
from the stem.

45

OF

˘of   is pronounced   ˘ov

‾ ˘   ˘   ˘   ˘   ‾ ˘
The damp mist of the fog
felt wet on my skin.

TO and DO

In these words the **o** says o̅o̅ (as in too).

to

do

If Ī must take a test, Ī try to do my best.

47

Introducing Double Consonants

What are the **consonant** letters in this word?

add

When two **consonant** letters are the **same** and stand **side - by - side** in a word, pronounce the **consonant sound** only **one** time.

I can add five plus five and
get a sum of ten.

Practice Words Using Double Consonants

) add

) buzz

) dress

) fuzz

) off

) yell

) egg

) tell

) Jill and Bill will do the task and try to
make less of a mess.

49

Soft Sound of S

Consonant s makes a **soft** sound and a **hard** sound.
When **s** is the **first letter** in a word, **s** makes a **soft** sound.

six   soft   stuff   sank

What is the **soft** sound of s?

Sam and Pam swam in the lake
at the same time.

When s comes after f, k, p or t, s makes a soft sound.

◡ huffs ◡ rusts ◠ sips ◠ dusts

◡ cuffs ◠ asks ◠ stuffs ◠ masks

◡ tests ◠ humps ◠ rests ◠ lumps

◡ Ken will not get lumps and bumps if he
◡ slips and trips on the soft sand.

Hard Sound of S

The **hard** sound of **s** is the sound of consonant **z**.
Listen, and hear the **hard** sound of **s**.

⟩ tubs

⟩ hugs

What is the **hard** sound of **s**?

⟩

⟩

⟩

⟩

⟩

⟩

Jeff gets a lot of hugs from
his mom and dad.

Practice Words Using the Hard Sound of S

is

beds

frills

as

bugs

hums

his

suds

hills

has

jugs

runs

Fred smiles as he makes his bed and hums as he scrubs the tub.

53

Exceptions to the "Silent E" Rule

You have learned that **e** at the end of a word makes the **first vowel** in the word make the **long vowel sound.**

Now you will learn some words that do not follow that rule.

In these words the first vowel is **short**:

give　　is pronounced　　**gĭv**

live　　is pronounced　　**lĭv**

have　　is pronounced　　**hăv**

Ĭ have lived by wet hills of sand and
Ī have lived by dry flat land.

In these words the o sounds like ŭ.

come is pronounced **kŭm**

some is pronounced **sŭm**

done is pronounced **dŭn**

love is pronounced **lŭv**

dove is pronounced **dŭv**

WAS and ONE

was is pronounced ‿ **wuz**

one is pronounced ‿ **wun**

‿ At one tīme ‿ Ī ‿ wȧs a tot and ‿ Ī ‿
Ī līked to run, skip, hop and trot.

57

LESSON 5 - READING CONSONANT COMBINATIONS

Read page 60 to your new reader.

Continue word building.

When your new reader has mastered the skills of this lesson, begin LESSON 6.

When these consonants stand

side - by - side in a word,

they combine to make a new sound.

Listen, and hear the new sound.

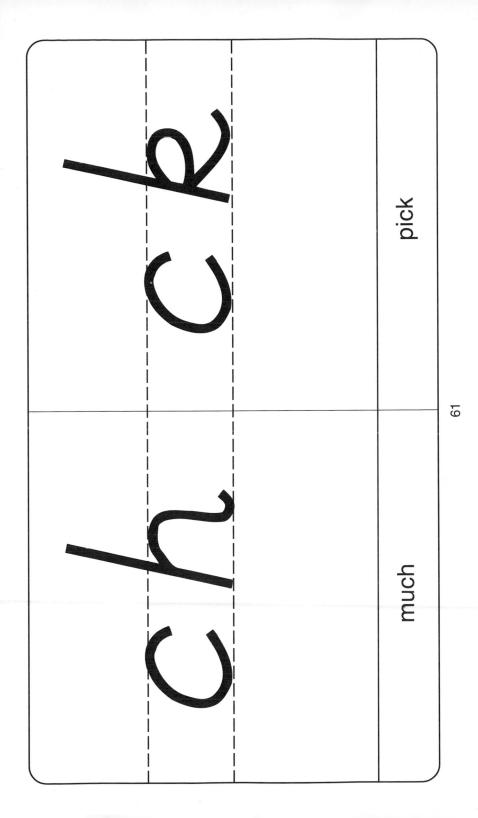

ch | ck

much | pick

61

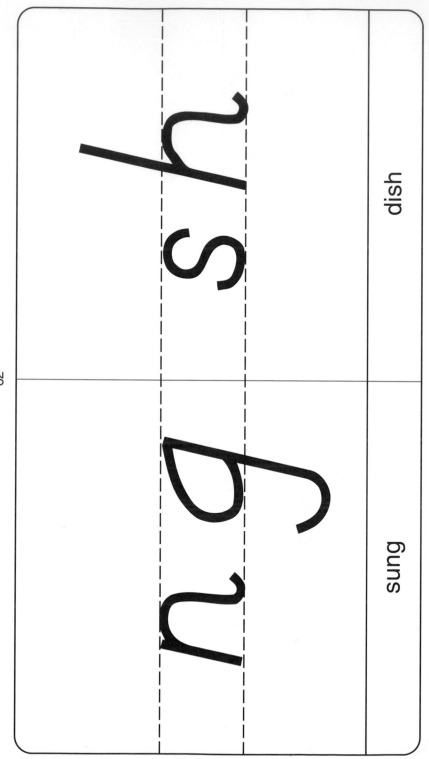

dish

sung

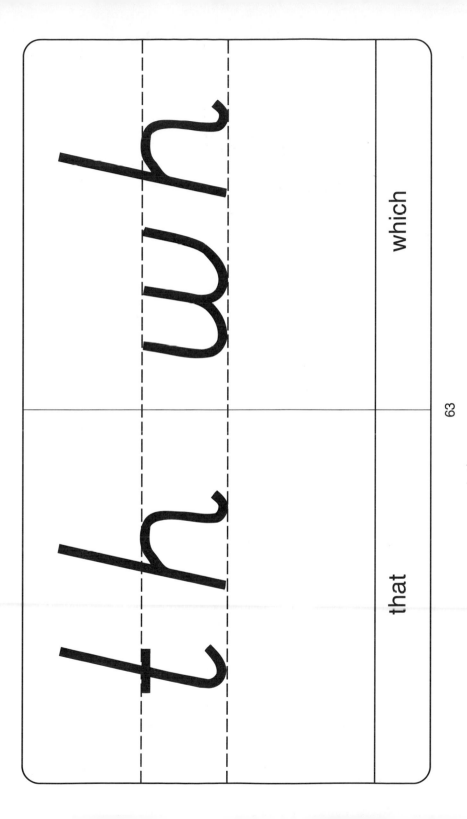

that

which

64

Practice Words Using the ch Combination

) much   ) bunch   ) such   ) lunch

‾ chase   ) bench   ) chest   ) pinch

) chill   ) chat   ) chunk   ) chap

) Ann and Bill had ‾ a) bunch) of) chips
) to munch at lunch.

Practice Words Using the ck Combination

( ) black

( ) block

( ) crack

( ) clock

( ) kick

( ) tuck

( ) pick

( ) yuck

( ) Nick

( ) peck

( ) trick

( ) neck

Tick - tock went the clock and
the time was nine.

Practice Words Using the ng Combination

rang   lung   sang   sung

king   bring   ping   string

spring   long   cling   song

The spring brings the songs of the
flocks on the wing.

Practice Words Using the sh Combination

) dāsh   ) dĭsh   ) măsh   ) wish

shy   shāke   shē   shāpe

shīne   ) crăsh   ) shrŭb   ) smăsh

The shāpe of the shrŭb was līke
the shĕll of a bĕll.

67

Practice Words Using the th Combination

(broth (thank (cloth (think

(this (that (these (those

(the (than (then (them

(The cloth felt as soft as the fluff of a muff.

Practice Words Using the wh Combination

ˌwhich

ˌwhack   ˉwhale   ˌwham

ˌwhy   ˌwhiz   ˉwhile   ˌwhen

ˌwhiff   ˉwhite   ˉwhine   ˌwhit

ˌDad ˉused a ˌwhisk to get the
ˌegg ˉwhites and milk to mix.

LESSON 6 - READING VOWEL COMBINATIONS

Read page 72 to your new reader.

Continue word building.

When your new reader has mastered the skills of this lesson, begin LESSON 7.

71

Most of the time, when two vowels stand

side - by - side in a word,

the first vowel makes the long vowel sound and

the second vowel is silent.

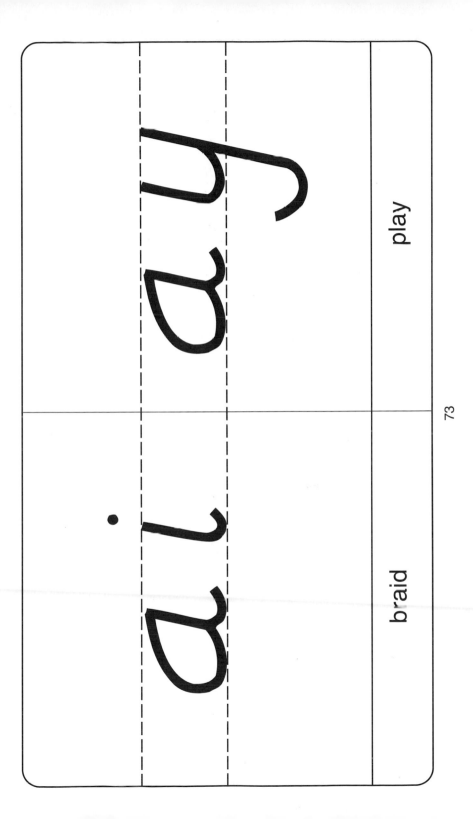

ay

play

ai

braid

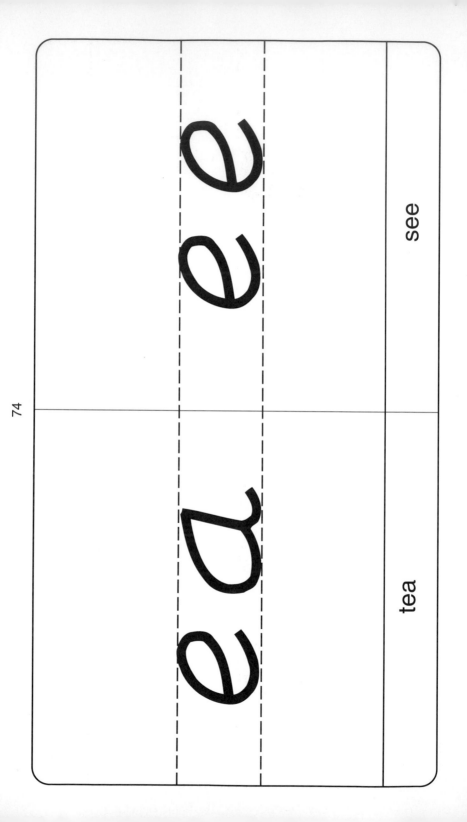

ea

tea

ee

see

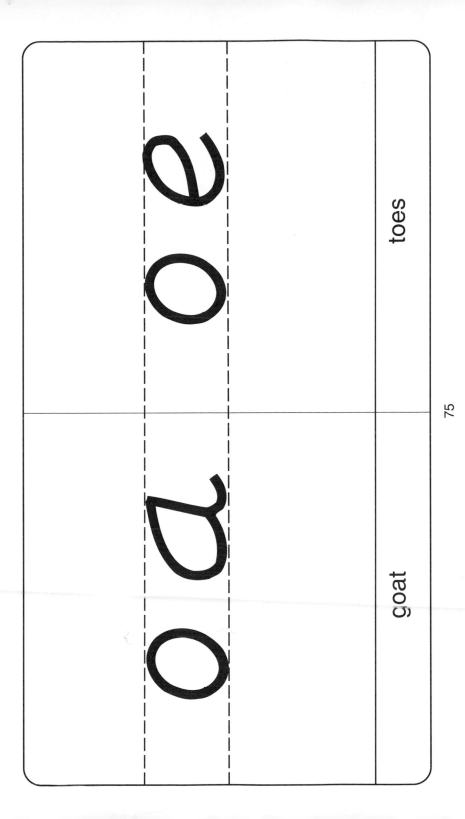

o a o e

goat

toes

Practice Words Using the ai Combination

braid drain laid grain

paint snail faint trail

brain bait strain wait

Jill can't wait till the fish bite the bait on the

end of the line on the pole.

Practice Words Using the ay Combination

clay	gray	may	play
stay	spray	sway	tray
pray	way	stray	jay

We may play with the clay if at the mat we stay.

77

Practice Words Using the ea Combination

beach   tea   teach   peas

Jean   each   team   peach

wheat   scream   cheat   dream

Jean had a dream that she ate a peach
as she sat on a rug at the beach.

Practice Words Using the ee Combination

cheese   sleep   freeze   sheep

tree   street   three   sweet

speed   sheet   breed   greet

From wee seeds come the grain of wheat,
the leaves of trees and the stick of weeds.

Practice Words Using the oa Combination

coach   float   roach   throat

load   toast   toad   roast

roar   goat   soar   boat

Three goats ate a load of hay and oats
and then had a nap by a tree of oak.

Practice Words Using the oe Combination

Jōe

gōes

hōe

tōes

Jōe ūses a hōe to dig up the weeds
when it's tīme to plant the seeds.

81

LESSON 7 - READING SPECIAL VOWEL COMBINATIONS

Read page 84 to ycur new reader.

Continue word building.

When your new reader has mastered the skills of this lesson, begin LESSON 8.

83

When these special vowels stand

side - by - side in a

word, they combine to make a new sound.

Listen, and hear the new sound.

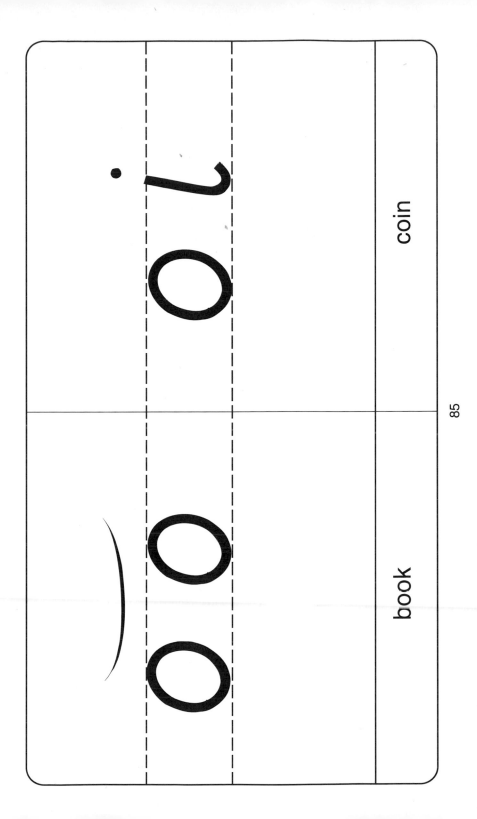

oi

coin

oo

book

85

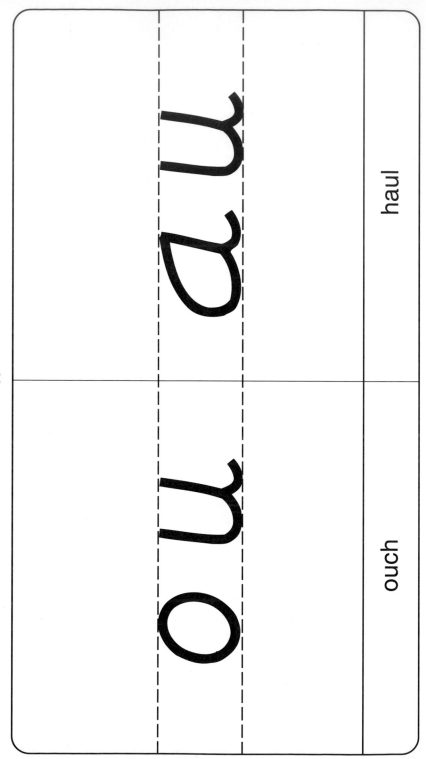

au   ou

haul   ouch

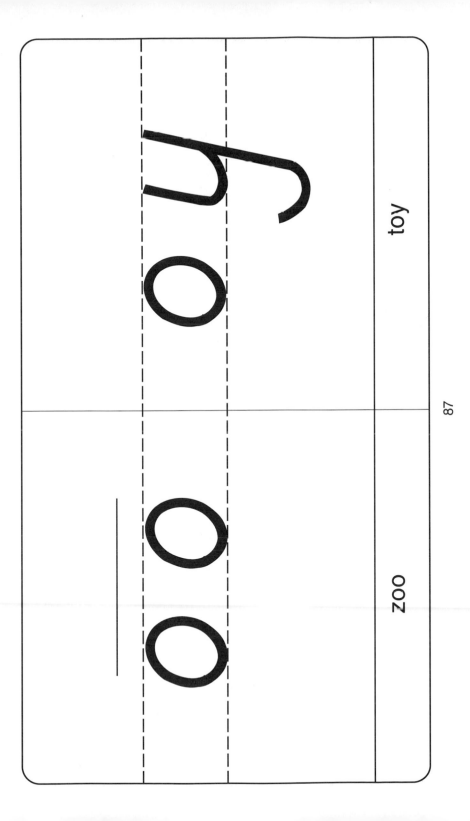

toy

zoo

Practice Words Using the Short oo Combination

book	good	hood
look	stood	wood
foot	cook	crook
	shook	soot

Ī love to sit by a long thin brook while Ī eat my snack and read a good book.

Practice Words Using the oi Combination

moist	noise	hoist	poise
joint	oil	point	coil
spoil	coin	broil	join

The spin of a drill makes the coal black oil rise up from the deep rich soil.

Practice Words Using the ou Combination

round	house	ground	mouse
grouch	out	couch	shout
ouch	proud	pouch	cloud

The mouse in our house made us shout
and jump up on the couch.

Practice Words Using the au Combination

fault

Paul

launch

haul

haunt

taunt

From the west coast to the east coast,
Paul drives a train that hauls grain.

Practice Words Using the Long oo Combination

moose   boo   goose   zoo

smooth   toot   tooth   root

droop   snoop   troop   scoop

Pete chased a goose on the loose and the
goose chose to roost on the roof.

Practice Words Using the oy Combination

Roy   boy   joy   toy

             boys   toys

Roy and the boys play with the toys and
then lay them up on the shelf.

93

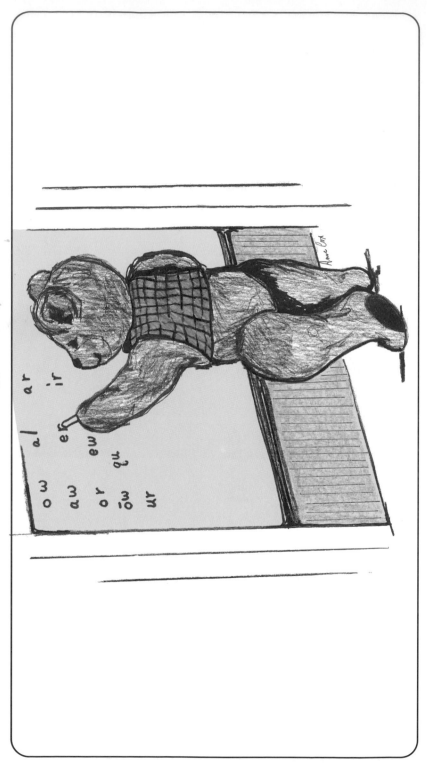

LESSON 8 - READING VOWEL-CONSONANT COMBINATIONS

Read page 96 to your new reader.

Continue word building.

95

When these vowels and consonants stand

side - by - side in a word,

they combine to make a new sound.

Listen, and hear the new sound.

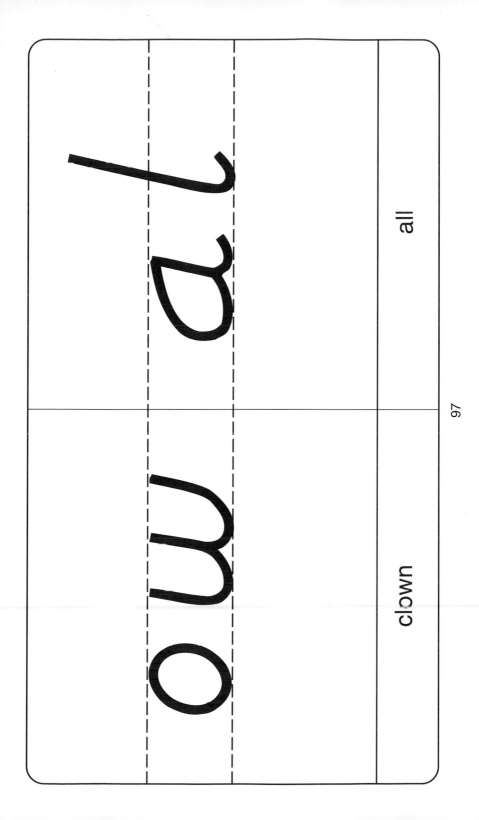

l

a

all

m

o

clown

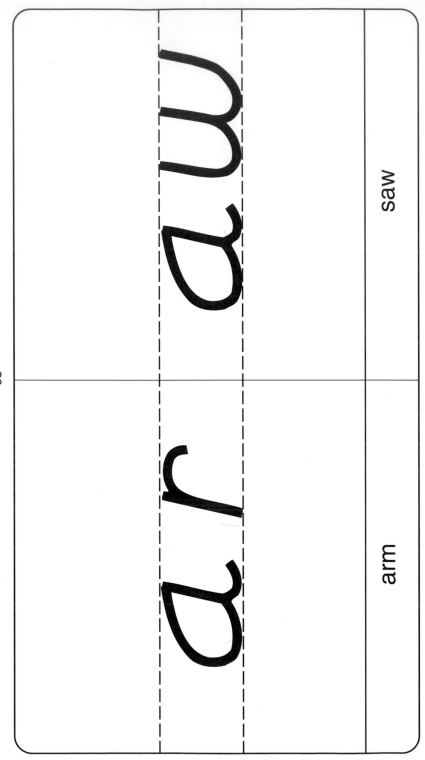

ar

arm

ma

saw

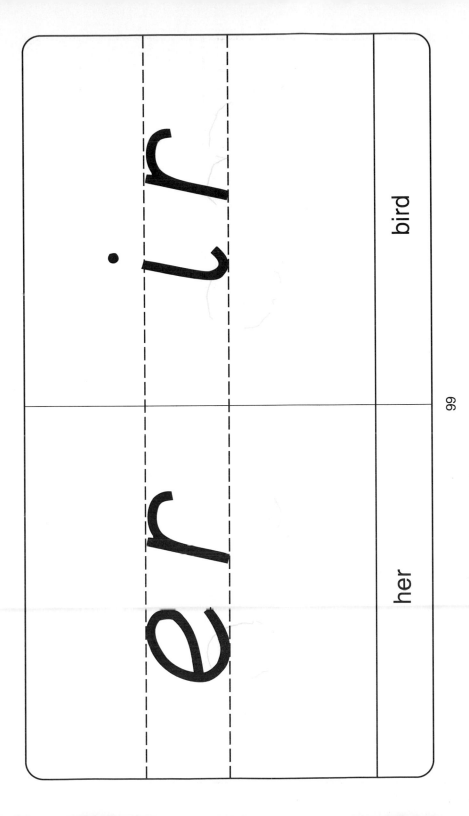

ir

bird

er

her

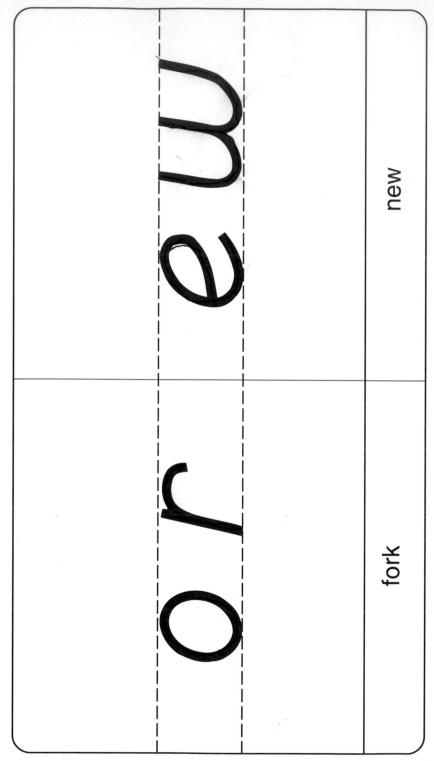

new

fork

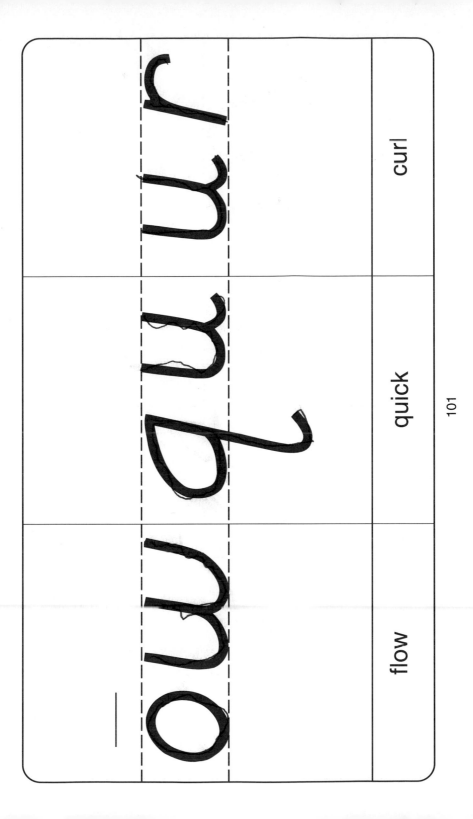

flow	quick	curl

Practice Words Using the Short ow Combination

brown	owl	growl
down	town	crown
fowl	cow	howl	now

The clown has a frown and a long green gown and a hat that droops on his crown.

Practice Words Using the al Combination

walk	salt	chalk	malt
all	small	ball	wall
stalk	stall	talk	mall

Ann stands tall and tries not to fall as she walks heel-to-toe on a small stone wall.

Practice Words Using the ar Combination

smart   shark   chart   spark

march   harp   arch   sharp

charm   marsh   farm   starch

In the clear dark sky of a cool March eve, the shine of the stars and the moon I see.

Practice Words Using the aw Combination

saw	yawn	drawn
crawl	claw	thaw
dawn	sprawl	shawl
	straw	bawl
		lawn
		shawl

Carl saw the paws of a fox, the claws of a hawk and the hoofs of a fawn at the zoo.

Practice Words Using the er Combination

jerk	serve	nerve
perch	fern	stern
herd	her	were

perk

clerk

Bert

Bert gets paid to bē a clerk in ā sweet-
shop and his job is to serve pie and pop.

Practice Words Using the ir Combination

first	girl	twirl
skirt	bird	thirst	third
birth	fir	shirt	stir
		chirp

The third black bird was the first to perch
and start to chirp on the branch of a birch.

Practice Words Using the *or* Combination

shore	torch	chore	porch
fork	short	cork	sport
thorn	more	horn	store

We went in the house and got off the porch

when a storm came in from the north.

Practice Words Using the ew Combination

chew	few	threw
screw	blew	drew	stew
crew	news	dew	chews

The dew on the grass at dawn makes
my feet wet as I walk on the lawn.

Practice Words Using the Long ow Combination

bōw	blōwn	shōwn
grōw	thrōwn	grōwn
bōwl	flōw	shōw
mōw		
snōw		
blōw		

The dēep blōwn snōw māde our drīve in the car a slōw gō.

Practice Words Using the qu Combination

quick   quail   quack   quill

squeeze   quit   squeak   quilt

A quail flies quick to the sound of a click
or the sound of a squeak or a quack.

111

Practice Words Using the ur Combination

church	curl	burst	hurl
spur	burn	purr	churn

A cat is sleek and soft and frail

and smiles when it purrs and curls its tail.

For information on how to order

PHONICS for the NEW READER

please write to:

WORDS PUBLISHING
P.O. Box 107
Firestone, Co. 80520-0107